OCEAN

ATLANTIC OCEAN

OCEAN

SOUTHERN OCEAN

Gone
Fishing

OCEAN LIFE BY THE NUMBERS

DAVID McLIMANS

WALKER & COMPANY · NEW YORK

For Benjamin

Special thanks to Patrick JB Flynn for helping me with this book

First published in the United States of America in 2008 by Walker Publishing Company, Inc.
Distributed to the trade by Macmillan

For information about permission to reproduce selections from this book, write to
Permissions, Walker & Company, 175 Fifth Avenue, New York, New York 10010

Library of Congress Cataloging-in-Publication Data
McLimans, David.
Gone fishing : ocean life by the numbers / David McLimans. — 1st ed.
p.   cm.
ISBN-13: 978-0-8027-9770-4 • ISBN-10: 0-8027-9770-9 (hardcover)
ISBN-13: 978-0-8027-9771-1 • ISBN-10: 0-8027-9771-7 (reinforced)
1. Marine animals—Juvenile literature. 2. Endangered species—Juvenile literature. I. Title.
QL122.2.M35 2008   591.77—dc22   2008014475

Typeset in Hoefler Text and Ocean Sans
Illustrations created using pencil, pen, brush, India ink, bristol board, and computer
Book design by David McLimans, Patrick JB Flynn, and John Candell

Visit Walker & Company's Web site at www.walkeryoungreaders.com

Printed in China
2 4 6 8 10 9 7 5 3 1 (hardcover)
2 4 6 8 10 9 7 5 3 1 (reinforced)

All papers used by Walker & Company are natural, recyclable products made from wood grown in well-managed forests.
The manufacturing processes conform to the environmental regulations of the country of origin.

Introduction

The ocean is vast, diverse, dynamic, amazing, and life giving. We once thought it was an unlimited resource, but today it is clear that the world's oceans are in trouble. Overfishing, pollution, loss of habitat, and climate change have all contributed to the current ecological crisis. We can no longer afford to ignore that the balance and health of the oceans affect the balance and health of our entire planet.

It is upsetting to read about the loss of ocean creatures and the habitats that support them. If we are to continue to coexist with nature, we must respect, repair, and nurture our wonderful blue planet. Our survival, and the lives of future generations, depends on restoring and maintaining the health of the oceans.

In this book I have used a variety of animals to show the diversity of sea life, particularly those whose forms fit naturally with the numbers one through ten. Some are officially considered endangered, some are experiencing population losses without being on the endangered list, and some are still thriving but living in threatened habitats.

There are many ways to help save the oceans and protect our beautiful blue planet. Start counting!

1 | African Penguin
Spheniscus demersus

CLASS: Aves

HABITAT: Coastal waters
and shorelines

AQUATIC REGIONS: Atlantic
and Indian oceans

THREATS: Habitat loss,
overfishing of food supply,
oil spills

STATUS: Vulnerable

CLASS: Mammalia

HABITAT: Throughout the oceans, but prefer near-shore and near-island habitats

AQUATIC REGIONS: Atlantic, Southern, Indian, and Pacific oceans; Arctic, Mediterranean, and Black seas

THREATS: Whaling, fishing nets, pollution, collisions with ships

STATUS: Vulnerable

CLASS: Cephalaspidomorphi

HABITAT: Open sea,
freshwater

AQUATIC REGIONS: Atlantic
Ocean, Mediterranean Sea,
Great Lakes

THREATS: Harvesting,
overfishing

STATUS: Not officially
endangered

CLASS: Actinopterygii

HABITAT: Open ocean and coastal regions near deep water

AQUATIC REGIONS: Atlantic, Pacific, and Indian oceans

THREATS: Overfishing, longline fishing

STATUS: Not officially endangered, but population has declined nearly 80 percent since the onset of longline fishing techniques

CLASS: Actinopterygii

HABITAT: Coral reefs, sea grass, submerged mangrove roots

AQUATIC REGIONS: Indian and Pacific oceans

THREATS: Coral reef destruction, capture for medical and scientific purposes, water pollution, overfishing

STATUS: Vulnerable

CLASS: Malacostraca

HABITAT: Coastal waters
and open ocean

AQUATIC REGION: Southern
Ocean

THREATS: Global warming,
harvesting for medical
purposes, industrial vacuum
fishing

STATUS: Not officially
endangered, but the
population may have
dropped as much as
80 percent since 1970

CLASS: Malacostraca

HABITAT: Mangrove roots, sandy or muddy beaches, salt marshes, intertidal zones

AQUATIC REGION: Atlantic and Pacific oceans

THREATS: Water pollution, loss of habitat, pet trade

STATUS: Not officially endangered

CLASS: Cephalopoda

HABITAT: Tide pools, coastal reefs

AQUATIC REGIONS: Pacific and Indian oceans

THREATS: Global warming, coral reef destruction

STATUS: Not officially endangered

Walrus
Odobenus rosmarus

CLASS: Mammalia

HABITAT: Open ocean over continental shelf, sea ice, pack ice, coastal islands

AQUATIC REGIONS: Arctic Ocean; Bering, Beaufort, and Chukchi seas

THREATS: Global warming, hunting

STATUS: Protected by the Marine Mammal Protection Act, but not officially endangered

CLASS: Aves

HABITAT: Grassland, open ocean

AQUATIC REGIONS: Atlantic, Indian, Pacific, and Southern oceans

THREATS: Longline fishing, trawl fishing

STATUS: Endangered

CLASS: Actinopterygii

HABITAT: Coral reefs, sandy flats, eel grass, rocky shorelines

AQUATIC REGIONS: Tropical waters throughout the world

THREATS: Global warming, habitat loss, coral bleaching, pet trade

STATUS: Not officially endangered

OCEAN FACTS

 Less than 1 percent of water on Earth is freshwater.

 In every fisherman's haul of shrimp, the nets catch up to 10 times the weight of the shrimp in other species, which is then trashed.

Giant kelp, the fastest-growing plant in the ocean, can grow up to 100 feet long in little more than a year.

 It takes about 1,000 years for a mass of seawater to make a complete lap around the globe.

 A gray whale migrates more than 10,000 miles a year, from the Bering Sea to Mexico, which is the longest migration of any mammal.

 It is estimated that there are more than 100,000 seamounts, undersea mountains often of volcanic origin, in the world's oceans.

Plastic waste kills up to 1 million seabirds every year.

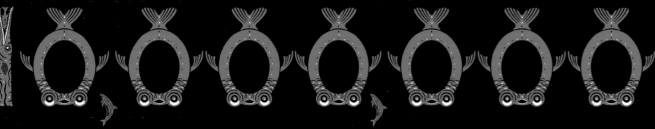

About 10 million shipping containers arrive in the United States each year.
Worldwide, about 10,000 containers fall overboard each year.

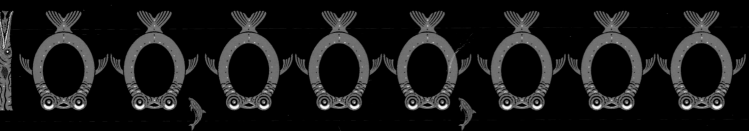

People slaughter up to 100 million sharks each year.

About 1 billion people live in coastal urban centers, and the resulting overdevelopment threatens almost 50 percent of the world's coastal habitats.

CLASS: Actinopterygii

HABITAT: Coastal waters and freshwater coastal streams

AQUATIC REGIONS: Atlantic Ocean

THREATS: Water pollution, habitat loss

STATUS: Not officially endangered

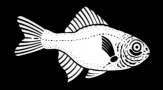

CLASS: Actinopterygii

HABITAT: Coral reefs, caves, deep ocean trenches

AQUATIC REGIONS: Pacific Ocean

THREATS: Global warming, coral bleaching

STATUS: Not officially endangered

CLASS: Mammalia

HABITAT: Rocky shorelines, beaches, sand pits

AQUATIC REGIONS: Atlantic Ocean and Mediterranean Sea

THREATS: Habitat loss, disease, human harvesting

STATUS: Critically endangered

CLASS: Actinopterygii

HABITAT: Abyssal plain, open ocean

AQUATIC REGIONS: Temperate and tropical oceans around the world

THREATS: Global warming, pollution, ocean acidification

STATUS: Not currently endangered; rarely seen by humans

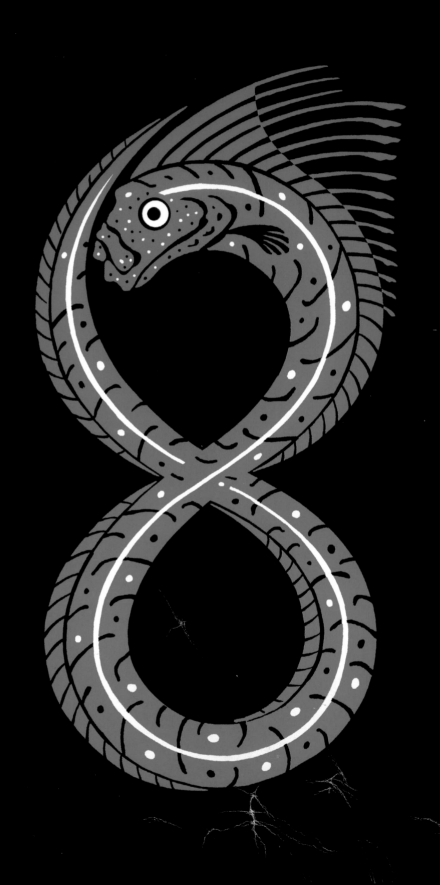

CLASS: Aves

HABITAT: Ocean shores, shallow coastal waters, estuaries, bays

AQUATIC REGIONS: Pacific and Atlantic oceans, Gulf of Mexico

THREATS: Oil spills, entrapment in fishing lines

STATUS: Removed from endangered species list in 1985 following recovery from DDT poisoning

6 | Great White Shark
Carcharodon carcharias

CLASS: Chondrichthyes

HABITAT: Coastal waters and open ocean

AQUATIC REGIONS: Atlantic, Pacific, and Indian oceans; Mediterranean and Black seas

THREATS: Hunting for sport and food

STATUS: Vulnerable

CLASS: Actinopterygii

HABITAT: Deep ocean

AQUATIC REGIONS: Tropical and temperate oceans around the world

THREATS: Very little is known about this species

STATUS: Not currently endangered

CLASS: Anthozoa

HABITAT: Coral reefs, caves, under rocky ledges and overhangs

AQUATIC REGIONS: Tropical waters of the Pacific Ocean and Red Sea

THREATS: Global warming, ocean acidification, pet trade

STATUS: Not currently endangered

CLASS: Mammalia

HABITAT: Shallow inshore waters, bays, lagoons, gulfs, estuaries, edge of continental shelf

AQUATIC REGIONS: Atlantic, Pacific, and Indian oceans; Mediterranean Sea

THREATS: Entrapment in fishing nets, pollution, hunting, boat collisions

STATUS: Not currently endangered, but protected by the Marine Mammal Protection Act

CLASS: Polychaeta

HABITAT: Deep ocean
hydrothermal vents

AQUATIC REGIONS: Pacific
Ocean

THREATS: Unknown; very
little is known about these
creatures

STATUS: Not currently
endangered

African Penguin

These graphic black-and-white flightless birds stand about two and a half feet (0.8 meters) tall and are the only penguins found in South Africa. They are fast swimmers and can maintain an average speed of 4.4 miles (7 kilometers) per hour—but up to 12 miles (20 kilometers) per hour if they are hunting. They breed on twenty-four offshore islands and three mainland sites found between Namibia and Port Elizabeth, South Africa. African penguins mate for life and often return to the same colony and nest year after year. In 1900 their population was at least 1.5 million. Their present population is about 180,000, about 10 percent of their original population.

Humpback Whale

This giant's heart alone weighs 430 pounds (195 kilograms). Humpback whales have two blowholes for breathing and can dive for as long as forty-five minutes. Full-grown adults can reach 53 feet (16 meters) in length and weigh 30–50 tons (27–45 metric tons). Whales have a unique pattern on the underside of their flukes, which can identify them like human fingerprints. They are well known for their ocean acrobatics and can be seen breaching (jumping out of the water), sky-hopping (poking their heads out of the water), and lobtailing (tail slapping). Humpback males are also known for their amazing and complex songs. It is believed there are 30,000–40,000 in the ocean today, only 30 to 35 percent of their original population.

Sea Lamprey

The sea lamprey is actually a primitive, jawless fish and not an eel. Sea lampreys are parasites that attach their round, horny-toothed sucker disks to fish, sucking the host dry before moving on to their next victim. They are ugly and unappetizing but were considered a delicacy during the Middle Ages. According to historians, King Henry I of England died from overstuffing himself on them. Sea lampreys were introduced as an alien species to the North American Great Lakes in 1929 and have since reduced the lake trout population significantly.

Blue Marlin

These huge, powerful, swift fish are spectacular jumpers. They are among the world's largest bony fish, and can grow to 10–13 feet (3–4 meters). They use their long, pointed, sharp bills to slash through schools of mackerel, tuna, skipjack, and frigate fish, and then return to devour the stunned and dead prey. These rare, solitary fish are always in motion and can easily cover 25–37 miles (40–60 kilometers) per day. They are ferocious fighters and are sought-after trophies by deep-sea fishermen. Marlin stock has been overfished for at least a decade and is being depleted faster than it can be replenished.

DEEPER

Tiger Tail Sea Horse

These tiny horselike creatures use their flexible tails to fasten themselves to plants and corals in reefs and lie in wait until their prey comes close. They can swivel their eyes independently of each other—giving them a wider view of approaching prey. Then they use their tubelike mouths to create a vacuum, sucking in small crustaceans and swallowing them whole. Females lay their eggs in a pouch located in the males' bellies, where they grow until the males "give birth" to adult-looking miniature sea horses. These monogamous creatures have been overfished and are listed as vulnerable.

Sand Fiddler Crab

Males have one larger front claw, up to 2 inches (5 centimeters) long, that looks a little like a fiddle. They wave it around in the air to attract females. If the large claw is broken off, the smaller claw will grow larger to take its place, while a new smaller claw grows to replace it. They live in colonies, and their burrows can be up to 2 feet (0.6 meters) deep. At high tide they will sometimes roll up a ball of sand and use it to plug up their burrow hole, trapping a small pocket of air inside for them to breathe while underwater. Shoreline development and water pollution spoil their environment.

Antarctic Krill

This tiny creature fuels the entire Antarctic food chain. Krill, which means "whale food" in Norwegian, are the food of choice for many fish, birds, and mammals. They gather in swarms that look red and can weigh 2 million tons (1.8 million metric tons) and spread over 280 square miles (450 square kilometers). Scientists estimate that the world's krill population outweighs all the people on Earth. Even so, superfishing trawlers now use giant hoses to pump krill out of the water at a staggering rate. Their numbers have dropped by as much as 80 percent since 1970, which could seriously upset the entire Antarctic ecosystem.

Blue-Ringed Octopus

This golf ball–size creature is very beautiful, but it also has enough powerful venom to kill a human in a matter of minutes. Bites occur only when they are picked out of the water or stepped on by accident. There is no known antidote for their poison, and the only treatment is hours of heart massage and artificial respiration until the toxin works its way out of the body. When resting, they are pale brown to yellow in color to blend into their environment. But when threatened, the body pales and electric blue rings glow intensely as a warning. These coral reef inhabitants are threatened by coral bleaching.

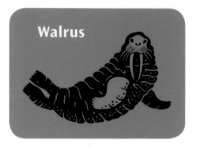

Walrus

These huge mammals hang out in large groups on sea ice, pack ice, or rocky islands in the Arctic. Both males and females have long, curved ivory tusks. These tusks are useful tools, enabling them to move their bodies along the ice, to break breathing holes in the ice when swimming beneath the ice pack, and for males to protect their harems. Hunters prize their ivory tusks and blubber oil. Still endangered by native hunters and poachers, melting sea ice now poses a new problem for walruses.

Atlantic Needlefish

These fierce-looking fish with rows of razor-sharp teeth were named for their pointed, elongated shape. They can jump out of the water when chasing prey. At night, they leap toward light and occasionally stab fishermen with their spearlike jaws. It is possible to see through the sides of their heads and look at their nervous systems and brains. Needlefish are not endangered, but sea grass, one of their favorite feeding habitats, is endangered worldwide because of water pollution.

Black-Browed Albatross

These seabirds get their name from the dark eyebrows that give them their angry, frowning look. They are gigantic birds with a wingspan of 7–8 feet (2.1–2.4 meters). They like to roam and seem to sail through the sky effortlessly on long, slender wings. When feeding, they plunge into the water and dive to catch fish, lobster, krill, and squid. Many are killed while they search for fish, getting caught by longline fisheries. When birds get caught on baited hooks, they are dragged underwater and drowned. This practice has led to a serious decline in the population.

Splitfin Flashlightfish

These remarkable fish come equipped with their own light source, which they can turn on and off as needed. The light comes from a bean-shaped area beneath its eye that contains bioluminescent, or glowing, bacteria. Like moths drawn to a flame, zooplankton and other tiny animals gather around the glowing eye and provide an easy meal. When spotted by a predator, the fish can cover the glowing bacteria with a special flap of muscle that raises and lowers like a window shade, then flee to safety in the darkness. The flashlight fish is not listed as endangered, but it lives in coral reef environments, which are endangered worldwide.

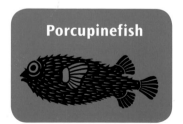

Porcupinefish

These amazing spiny fish fill themselves with air or water and become unappetizing balls with spikes to ward off predators. Then, when any threats have passed, they float upside down until they can release the extra air and return to their normal flat shape and swimming position. Their teeth are fused together into beaks that are able to crack the shells of snails, sea urchins, and crabs. Their skin is semitoxic and may be fatal if eaten.

These trusting sea mammals have lived near people since the times of the ancient Greeks, who considered them a sign of luck and pictured them on early coins. Ancient Romans, however, were more interested in hunting them for their pelts—which made tents, shoes, and cloth—and their fat, which was used for oil lamps, candles, and medicine. Their population began a steep decline during the Roman era and today they have become one of the six most endangered mammals in the world. They seek refuge in hidden underwater caves, with entrances that are unseen from above the waterline. Scientists believe that fewer than six hundred monk seals survive today.

Oarfish are rare, solitary, narrow sea creatures and are the longest of all bony fish, growing up to 25 feet (7.6 meters) in length. Sometimes called "the king of the herrings," this strange, exotic-looking monster has a bright red crest and may be responsible for sea serpent sightings like the Loch Ness monster. They are not listed as endangered or vulnerable, but little is known about them because sightings are very rare, and only a few stranded dead specimens have been found and examined.

Dynamic divers and fish eaters, brown pelicans have 18-inch (45.7-centimeter) bills, the longest of any bird. From as high as 70 feet (21.3 meters), they can spot a single fish with their keen eyesight. Then they partially fold their wings and dive straight down to the water—scooping the fish and up to 3 gallons (11.4 liters) of water into their enormous expandable throat pouch. When they surface, they drain the water and eat the fish that are left behind. These seabirds became endangered mainly from the use of DDT, which caused their eggshells to thin and break. Since DDT was banned in 1972, brown pelicans have been making a comeback.

Great whites are the largest predatory fish in the sea, 15 feet (4.6 meters) in length on average, and their mouths are lined with 3,000 serrated, triangular teeth arranged in rows. The movie *Jaws* gave great whites a bad reputation as man eaters. In fact, scientists have determined that attacks on humans are almost always accidental. The same cannot be said about humans attacking great whites. They have made it onto the "Ten Most Wanted" list, issued by the World Wildlife Foundation, as one of the most hunted animals in the wild—for their fins and teeth and the hunter's bragging rights.

These fierce-looking fish live at 8,000 feet (2,438 meters) or more and could be right out of Jules Verne's novel *20,000 Leagues Under the Sea.* With fangs too big for their mouths, and jaws that can open to an angle wider than ninety degrees, viperfish are able to catch and swallow fish that are much bigger than they are. Their eyes are very large to utilize what little light there is in the deep sea. Viperfish also have twenty-four or more bioluminescent photophores glowing along their bodies, most likely used to communicate with other viperfish and to attract prey. Very little is known about these strange deep-sea creatures.

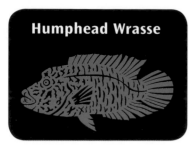

Humphead Wrasse

With massive lips and canine teeth, these giant fish—which can grow up to 7.5 feet (2.3 meters) long—are able to crunch through a variety of toxic reef creatures, including the spiky crown-of-thorn starfish, without getting sick. But those powerful lips also put them in danger. Wealthy Asian diners are willing to pay up to $400 for a single serving of wrasse lips—and up to $10,000 for an entire fish. Many of these unusual fish begin as females but turn into males later in life, though scientists don't know how they do this. Giant wrasse have been hunted to the brink of extinction.

Bottlenose Dolphin

These powerful swimmers seem so at home in the water that it's easy to forget they are mammals that need to surface every five to eight minutes for air. They need to be awake or semiconscious to breathe or else they will drown. Luckily, they have the unusual ability to rest one half of their brain at a time, while the other half stays awake to breathe and watch for danger. Dolphins communicate with each other through a series of clicks, squeaks, and high-frequency whistles. They also use these clicks to steer through the ocean, an ability known as "echolocation."

Carnation Coral

Though you may think these creatures are plants, they are actually living animals. They are also known as "cauliflower coral" because of their shape. They come in a variety of vibrant colors, with red and orange the most common. Coral reefs are home to more kinds of life than any other marine habitat. But that diversity is being threatened as the corals are under attack from a variety of sources. Global warming is causing coral bleaching, and waves from increasingly severe storms damage coral reefs.

Giant Tube Worm

When oceanographers discovered large groups of giant worms—some as long as 10 feet (3.05 meters)—living near geothermal vents at depths of 8,000 feet (2,438 meters), they were astounded. This discovery completely changed their concept of life because these tube worms don't depend on the sun to produce their food source, as in photosynthesis, but have developed a symbiotic relationship with bacteria from the deep-sea vents. The bacteria turn chemicals into food in a process called chemosynthesis. Tube worms have no mouths, eyes, or stomachs. When they extend their bright red plumes to take in bacteria, they look like giant lipsticks.

OUR BLUE PLANET

～～～～～～～～

There are five oceans on our planet. In size order they are:

Pacific: 64.0 million square miles (165.7 million square kilometers)

Atlantic: 31.8 million square miles (82.4 million square kilometers)

Indian: 28.3 million square miles (73.4 million square kilometers)

Southern: 7.8 million square miles (20.3 million square kilometers)

Arctic: 5.4 million square miles (14.1 million square kilometers)

The planet's longest mountain range is on the ocean floor. The Mid-Atlantic Ridge stretches from pole to pole and is part of the submerged mountain range that stretches for 40,000 miles (65,000 kilometers), circling the entire globe.

90 percent of the planet's volcanic activity occurs in the ocean.

An estimated 80 percent of Earth's living creatures are found in and around the oceans.

71 percent of Earth's surface is covered by oceans, and those oceans equal 97 percent of the total water on Earth.

Less than 5 percent of all the oceans have been explored by humans.

OCEAN THREATS BY THE NUMBERS

- There are 220,000 pounds of garbage swirling out in the **Great Pacific Garbage Patch**, and it is growing every year. This "garbage soup" is made up of everything we have dumped into the oceans. Scientists now believe it is twice the size of Texas. Tides carry the garbage into two separate areas, on either side of the Hawaiian Islands. Unfortunately there are similar patches in the Atlantic and Indian oceans, though they are much smaller.

- **Plastic** accounts for up to 80 percent of all the debris in the oceans—and endangers all the animals and plants that live there. Every square mile of ocean contains approximately 46,000 pieces of plastic.

- Lost or abandoned fishing nets, called **ghost nets**, create problems for many marine animals and seabirds—including protected species. Animals that are caught can starve and drown. These discarded nets entangle northern fur seals, killing as many as 20,000 annually.

- There are 200 **Dead Zones** in the world's oceans, and they are growing every year. Oxygen levels in the water drop so low in these areas that it is difficult, if not impossible, for marine plants and animals to survive. Scientists believe that sewage, fertilizer and other chemical runoff from rivers, and climate change are contributing to the problem. The Gulf of Mexico dead zone, off the coast of Louisiana and Texas, is the largest. It varies in size every year, but it is usually between 6,000 and 7,000 square miles (9,656 and 11,265 square kilometers). In August 2007 it was 7,900 square miles—about the size of the state of New Jersey!

To learn more about organizations that help the oceans, check out these Web sites:

ANTARCTIC KRILL CONSERVATION PROJECT:
www.krillcount.org

BLUE OCEAN INSTITUTE: www.blueocean.org

CONSERVE OUR OCEAN LEGACY: www.oceanlegacy.org

EARTH TRUST: http://earthtrust.org

ENVIRONMENTAL DEFENSE FUND: www.edf.org

GREENPEACE: www.greenpeace.org

INTERGOVERNMENTAL OCEANOGRAPHIC COMMISSION:
http://ioc.unesco.org/iocweb/index.php

IUCN, THE WORLD CONSERVATION UNION:
www.iucnredlist.org

MARINE BIO: www.marinebio.org

MARINE CONNECTION: www.marineconnection.org

MONTEREY BAY AQUARIUM:
http://montereybayaquarium.org

OCEAN VOYAGER: www.oceanvoyager.org

PEW OCEANS COMMISSION:
www.pewtrust.org/our_work.aspx?category=126

REEF RELIEF: www.reefrelief.org

SAVE OUR SEAS: www.saveourseas.org

SHEDD AQUARIUM: www.sheddaquarium.org

SIERRA CLUB: www.sierraclub.org

STARFISH: www.starfish.ch

UNITED NATIONS ATLAS OF THE OCEANS:
www.oceansatlas.org

WILDERNESS SOCIETY: www.wilderness.org

WOODS HOLE OCEANOGRAPHIC INSTITUTION:
www.whoi.edu

WORLD WILDLIFE FUND: www.panda.org

For further reading:

American Museum of Natural History. *Ocean: The World's Last Wilderness Revealed.* New York: DK Publishing, 2006.

Ballesta, Laurent and Pierre Descamp. *Planet Ocean: Voyage to the Heart of the Marine Realm.* Washington DC: National Geographic, 2007.

Cole, Joanna and Bruce Degen. *The Magic School Bus on the Ocean Floor.* New York: Scholastic, 1994.

Doubilet, David. *Fish Face.* London, England: Phaidon Press, 2007 (new edition).

Earle, Sylvia. *National Geographic Atlas of the Ocean.* Washington DC: National Geographic, 2001.

Earle, Sylvia. *Hello, Fish: Visiting the Coral Reef.* Washington DC: National Geographic, 2001.

Griffin Burns, Loree. *Tracking Trash: Flotsam, Jetsam, and the Science of Ocean Motion.* Boston: Houghton Mifflin, 2007.

Hutchinson, Stephen and Lawrence E. Hawkins. *Oceans: A Visual Guide.* Ontario, Canada: Firefly Books, 2005.

Nye, Bill. *Bill Nye the Science Guy's Big Blue Ocean.* New York: Hyperion, 2003.

Scubazoo. *Reef.* New York: DK Publishing, 2007.

Woodward, John. *Oceans Atlas: An Amazing Aquatic Adventure.* New York: DK Publishing, 2007.